All You Need to Know to Become an Entrepreneur

I0473187

THERONE SHELLMAN

This is a work of nonfiction. In most cases the names of people and locales have been changed to protect their identities.

Institutions, libraries and bookstores can purchase books at 50% off retail price. Please contact us for in info.

Printed in the United States of America
10 9 8 7 6 5 4 3 2 1

10 ISBN#: 978-1475174212
13 ISBN#: 1475174217
LCCN:

Therone Shellman Book Consulting

www.theroneshellman.com
www.myspace.com/theroneshellman
www.blogtalkradio.com/keepingitreal
Editor: Melissa Forbes/Carbon Copy Editing
Graphics Designer: Marsha Porter/Mahoganie Underground

TABLE OF CONTENTS

INTRODUCTION

Looking back upon my life, now at the age of 39 years old I realize now more than ever the burning desire to become an entrepreneur has been with me since I obtained my first job as a teen. I was only in Junior High School then, but the accumulation of wealth was clearly on my mind, as my eyes set upon the pay envelope at the end of each week.

The difference between my understanding of wealth as a teen and now is in myself and what place I play in how to go about accumulating wealth. At the age of 14-15 years old it never occurred to me it was possible for me to own my own business. In fact I do not remember actually seeing an African American owned business, or coming across an African American who claimed to be a business owner. But then again I resided in Long Island, N.Y. which is one of the most segregated places to live within the U.S. Needless to say African Americans have always been underrepresented in the business and political community.

It would be years later while incarcerated that the idea of writing books and entrepreneurship seemed like an achievable possibility. Being incarcerated with other African Americans who resided within other geographic locations of the state of New York, and boroughs of NYC. I became open to the reality a lot of African Americans were in fact business owners.

By my early twenties, entrepreneurism was deeply implanted in my psyche. But I was still somewhat crippled by my heredity and past social beliefs which I gained through others. I lacked financial literacy because I grew up poor and was taught to be poor.

Without the necessary proper guidance I made critical mistakes as a teen which would affect me for many years, over a decade to be exact.

It would not be until I reached the Age of twenty eight that I would find my life somewhat free from turmoil to allow myself to begin to set a definite plan. Entrepreneurship is what keeps the economy and the world going. But the occupation entails so many skills which people lack and most are not willing to take the time to seek and learn.

In my purpose of writing "All You Need to Know to Become an Entrepreneur" my motivation was not solely based upon being an entrepreneur and looking as the work as an investment. I also looked at the work fulfilling my need to do the best I can with my endeavor to write and put fourth for the public quality work. Helping others is probably the best service one can render to mankind besides helping oneself. Therefore let's say this book is a labor for profit as a business investment and a service to help my fellow humans.

Most of what has been written within this book has been researched for several years. This work is both a product of personal experience, and what I've learned via internet, book study and watching others in business.

At the time of this writing I'm nowhere near wealthy in the monetary sense, but my experiences and learning have rendered me wealthy by far in knowledge. In the process of obtaining monetary wealth, most of us will have to shed our old learning, re-educate ourselves, commit to study before we can actually go about the accumulation of material wealth.

To not go through the steps will in most cases in the long run bring disaster. There is a saying which states, "A fool with money will be a fool without sooner or later." I believe it goes something like that. The bottom-line is that if you ask most people who have developed wealth and lost through business matters, if you were to ask them to be honest and tell you why they lost their fortune they would tell you in so many words it was because of their lack of certain education, and their failure to do certain duties. Knowledge is the foundation, and without it one cannot obtain and maintain anything.

I've been in business for myself for five years now. All of the years have been spent learning, accumulating knowledge and wealth, bumping my head, making mistakes, losing wealth and learning through temporary failure and defeat. It isn't until now that I feel I'm prepared to move forward and obtain my definite purpose. There will be many more business books to come but "All You Need to Become an Entrepreneur" shall give you a head start over myself, and others who have learned by just stepping out into the world and doing it without knowing right or wrong. All I knew was that I was and am meant to do more in life than to have my existence and future dictated by others. Hopefully you feel the same.

DEDICATION

Well, my ability to think and reason I owe to one source, and this is to our Creator who I'm forever indebted to. Trading and entrepreneurship can be traced all the way back to B.C. The spirit of entrepreneurship resided in my genetic makeup long before I was physically manifested.

Illegally working as a teen under aged awakened the spark in me to have a desire to not just accumulate physical wealth, but also understand that wealth and power go hand in hand. I have to thank my first employers for awareness that one needs to work for whatever they seek.

Toward my late teens into my early twenties I was blessed to come across such business books as, One Minute Manager, 7 Habits of Highly Effective People and from there the search was on to figure out how I was going to put the pieces together and forge my destiny. So for all the teachers and writers throughout the ages who have manifested their thoughts and poured their energies out into the universe I'm grateful because, I've learned and felt all of your callings.

My personal experiences are vast and many. From the school of hard knocks and the streets, to various jobs ranging from menial to supervising others I've had the ability and privilege to learn within many realms of life.

To all you entrepreneurs, dead or alive it is your spirit which compelled me to not be scared and act upon the capabilities our Creator has bestowed me with.

If I had to mention one single person who has influenced or impressed upon me the most I would have to say Napoleon Hill. The Law of Success up to this very date has been the best work I've read detailing how to become successful. His descriptive detail of how individuals like Henry Ford have become successful has convinced me beyond truth that there is a master plan in regards to obtaining success.

Put your thinking cap on and enjoy the ride.

Have you ever thought about becoming an entrepreneur?

- Are you a leader?
- Are you confident?
- Are you organized?
- Do you have unique services, skills, or products to offer?
- Are you a risk taker?
- Are you willing to make sacrifices now to obtain more down the road?
- Do you have the necessary experience, and an interest in the type of business you would like to open?

If you answered yes to the above questions, then owning your own business may be the right choice for you. Businesses are born from ideas. Entrepreneurs have a vision and develop a mission that leads to goals, which are fueled by a strategy to seek success.

Part 1: Basic Types of Business Structures

A. Sole Proprietorship.

A sole proprietorship is a business owned by one individual, and it is not incorporated. It is the easiest business structure to establish, but it provides the least amount of protection to the owner. All business liabilities become the owner's personal liabilities. All income and expenses of the business are placed on the owner's personal income tax return. As a sole proprietor, the owner may be liable for income taxes, self employment taxes, Social Security, and Medicare taxes (FICA).

Disadvantages:
1. The owner is personally liable for all business's debts, and liability is not limited to the value of the business. The owner is personally liable for any and all debt incurred.
2. It is usually more difficult to borrow money or obtain outside investment with a sole proprietorship than with other types of business structures.
3. If the owner becomes ill for any reason, the business is likely to fail.
4. All management responsibility is with the owner.

Establishing a Sole Proprietorship:
In order to establish a sole proprietorship, the owner should:
1. Obtain local business licenses.
2. Check on local zoning ordinances, regulations, and other land use restrictions.
3. Determine if your particular business requires a state license to operate. Find out if any federal permits or licenses are required.
4. File with your appropriate county official for the business name, then file an affidavit of

publication. These guidelines apply to almost all states. Please check with your county clerk to make sure you are adhering to your states rules.

5. Locate a good insurance agent to obtain fire, accident, liability, and theft insurance. You may operate your business out of your home and have no employees. Yet there is a possibility that a fire occurs, or some of your property is stolen. So when making the decision as to whether or not you need insurance and how much that you're going to need take your time to think things through and take everything into account.

6. Obtain an accountant. All profits and losses from the business are to be reported on your personal income tax.

When you file the paperwork with the county clerk to conduct business under any name other than your own, your business becomes known as, for example, John Smith d/b/a (doing business as) Acme Plumbing. You must file paperwork to obtain a d/b/a name if you wish to open a bank account under any name other than your own.

B. Partnership

A general partnership is similar to doing business as a sole proprietor except there are more than one owner has partners with whom to share the business's losses and gains. The owners do not have the same liability protection as with a corporation or limited liability company, but a partnership is a fast way to get a business started.

Advantages:
1. Partnerships are basically as easy to establish as sole proprietorships.
2. The profits from the business flow directly through to the partners personal tax returns.
3. You don't have to register with your state and pay a fee, as you do to establish a corporation or limited liability company.

Disadvantages:
1. Partnerships may have different business objectives and visions.
2. Business debts and liabilities the partners are personally liable for.
3. Each partner's commitments to the business may not be equal.
4. Personal quarrels may occur.

Establishing a Partnership:
In order to establish a partnership, the owners should:
1. Obtain local business licenses.
2. Check on local zoning ordinances, regulations, and other land use restrictions.
3. Determine if your particular business requires a state license to operate. Find out if any federal permits or licenses are required.
4. File with your appropriate county official for the business name, then file an affidavit of publication. These guidelines apply to almost all states. Please check with your county clerk to make sure you are adhering to your states rules.
5. Get an EIN Employee Identification Number from IRS using form SS-4.

6. Draft written agreement between the partners determining a financial plan, management responsibilities, day to day activities, etc.

7. Locate a good insurance agent to obtain fire, accident, liability, and theft insurance. You may operate your business out of your home and have no employees. Yet there is a possibility that a fire occurs, or some of your property is stolen. So when making the decision as to whether or not you need insurance and how much that you you're your time to think things through and take everything into account.

8. Obtain an accountant. All profits and losses from the business are to be reported on your personal income tax.

When you file the paperwork with the county clerk to conduct business under any name other than your own, your business becomes known as, for example, John Smith d/b/a (doing business as) Acme Plumbing. You must file paperwork to obtain a d/b/a name if you wish to open a bank account under any name other than your own.

C. S Corporation

An S Corp is a special type of corporation, of particular interest to sole proprietorships or partners. An entrepreneur who is interested in incorporating his or her business to limit personal liability assets may choose to do so through an S Corp. The S Corp allows the entrepreneur to protect his or her assets in the event of business failure. A simple sole proprietorship or partnership does not provide this protection.

Advantages:
1. The S corporation has shareholders and is taxed like a sole proprietorship or partnership.
2. The owner has the protection of limited liability without having to pay corporate taxes.
3. The corporation is a separate legal entity. This means a corporation can open a bank account, own property, and do business under the corporation's name, protecting the owner's personal name.
4. Earnings of an S Corporation—after paying a reasonable salary to the shareholders—can be passed through as distributions of profits, and are not subject to self-employment taxes.

Disadvantages:
1. S Corps are not treated the same in every state. In some states an S Corp is treated like any other corporation regarding tax liability. It is important to seek professional advice before committing to set up an S corp. I placed this in the disadvantage area because S Corps in general are not the same size companies as C Corps which are publicly traded and revenue is much greater.
2. There are restrictions on who can be owners (shareholders) of an S Corporation. An S Corporation can have no more than seventy-five shareholders, and none of the shareholders can be non-resident aliens. Also, shareholders cannot be other corporations or LLCs.

Establishing an S Corp:
To form an S Corp you must file articles of incorporation with the Secretary of State. An S Corp is formed by filing incorporation documents with your state's department of state, department of corpora-

tions, or other appropriate department. Once the business has incorporated, the owners may decide to file taxes as an S Corporation.

D. Limited Liability Company (LLC)

An LLC is a type of company, authorized to exist only in certain states, whose owners and managers receive the limited liability and (usually) tax benefits of an S Corporation without having to conform to the S Corporation restrictions.

Advantages:
1. The LLC allows for multiple owners or members. Additionally, there is a managing member who also enjoys the rewards of limited liability, and is typically the person responsible for managing the business.
2. The profits or losses of the business pass directly through to the owner's personal income tax return on Form 1040. The LLC files a Form 1065, and then lists each member's taxable profit on Form K-1. In other words, the LLC does not file taxes.
3. An LLC offers greater flexibility in ownership and ease of operation. The owners of an LLC can distribute profits in any manner they see fit. For example, you and a partner are owners of an LLC. Your partner contributed forty thousand dollars for capital. You only contributed ten thousand dollars, but you perform 90 percent of the work. The two of you decide that, in the interest of fairness, you will split the profits evenly, meaning you will get 50 percent and your partner will receive 50 percent. This is possible to do with an LLC, whereas other business structures do not allow such flexibility.

Disadvantages:

1. Earnings of most members are generally subject to self-employment tax. There are other disadvantages that should be researched. LLC is the newest of all the business structures, so you will need an experienced tax professional to explain all its details.
2. There is not one guideline which governs how Limited Liability Companies operate within all states. So if an LLC conducts business within many states there is a possibility it may not receive the same treatment.
3. Conversion of an existing business to LLC company status could result in tax recognition on appreciated assets.
4. Not all businesses can be formed as an LLC. Businesses in trust and insurance and banking are in most instances prohibited from forming an LLC.
5. In California, accountants, architects, lawyers, doctors and other licensed healthcare professionals are restricted from forming their business as a LLC.

Establishing an LLC:

1. Choose an available business name.
2. File articles of organization and pay filing fee which can range anywhere from $100 to $800.
3. Obtain any licenses and permits your business needs. The licenses all depend on the type of business you're starting.
4. Publish your notice of intent to form an LLC (this is only required within a few states). Check with your accountant, attorney or the business organization that you're seeking to assist you with forming your LLC.

There are several business savvy websites like legalzoom.com, and limitedliabilitycompanycenter.com, sba.gov, no-lo.com, irs.gov, incorporate.com and bizfiling.com so get on your pc and get going. There is a saying which is so true, "A man who fails plan plans to fail".

Part 2: Writing a Business Plan

A business plan is a carefully thought out docu-
ment detailing the steps you will take to develop a
financially successful business. Preparing your
business plan will help you think through every aspect
of your business. If your proposed business needs
investors or a loan, the first thing lenders want to see
is a business plan.

A business plan will serve as an assessment tool.
As you work through the points in your plan, you can
fix or reevaluate your ideas. Once your business is up
and running, your business plan will help you keep on
track and move forward to the goals you established
when first thinking about the business.

Your business plan should consist of four to six
sections: introduction or executive summary, marketing analyses, financial management, operations or
strategy and implementation, mission statement and
concluding statement. Below are short descriptions of
each part of a business plan. Again there is no written
rule in stone as to what titles you need to give each
section, but it is a must that you cover everything
from what you and your company are about to how it
operates or will operate, financial history if any or
future projections, marketing and how you plan to
grow the company. I have also included the business
plan I wrote for establishing a bookstore/kiosk
division of Third Eye Publishing, Inc.

Introduction: Provide a detailed description of the
business and its goals. Discuss the legal structure and
ownership. Explain your experience and skills, and
list the advantages your business and you have over
the competition.

Marketing: Explain the products and services being

offered. Identify the demographics of the customer base, i.e., its race, age, gender, etc. Explain the marketing and publicity you plan to use. Give an outline of your pricing strategy.

Financial Management: Include personal financial statements and income statement projections for the first three years of your business.

Business Operations: Provide an outline and schedule of all business activities with a description of hours and days of operation, equipment and supplies that are needed, as well as how inventory will be maintained.

Concluding Statement: In your concluding statement you will briefly summarize all the information in each section of your business plan to give an overall analysis of why you feel your business venture will be successful.

Sample Business Plan
Third Eye Books & Things
(Bookstore and vending division of Third Eye Publishing, Inc.)

Business Plan
1.0   Executive Summary
Rationale:

More young African Americans are reading now than ever before in the history of the United States. With the rebirth of urban literature and stories that take place within urban settings, this genre has become one of the fastest growing markets in the book industry. In suburban areas most of the bookstores are large chain retail stores like Borders and Barnes & Noble that carry a very small selection of African American books. As an author I've toured most of the urban cities within the northeastern states and I've asked many of the store clerks who represents most of their customer base. I was surprised to find out that most of them told me African American women. I found this to be even the case for libraries in urban areas where I asked and would receive the same response from clerks.

Third Eye Publishing, Inc. currently has two titles published, another releasing on November 20, 2007, and one more releasing December 15, 2007. Third Eye Books & Things will serve as a distribution center for Third Eye Publishing, Inc. (www.thirdeyepublishing.org   and www.myspace.com/theroneshellman)

Objective:

Third Eye Books & Things will be the bookstore/kiosk and vending division of Third Eye Publishing, Inc. It will carry Third Eye Publishing book titles and other African American titles, as well as children books, financial health literature, natural health and beauty products like soaps, face cream, Shea butter, lotions, and other paraphernalia such as posters and buttons.

Its store market emphasis will be to exist as a satellite store (a booth or kiosk approximately ten feet by twelve feet) within a local flea market/mall location where there is a large customer base and the store overhead will be much lower than a store front in the mall. This location will serve as the headquarters for Third Eye Publishing, Inc.'s distribution operations.

1.1   Mission

Third Eye Books & Things will develop into the premier location for local Long Island residents to buy African American books and natural healthcare products. Currently most Long Island customers cater to the street vendor market in such areas as Jamaica Avenue (Queens, New York, 125th Street in Harlem, New York). These areas are twenty-five to thirty-five miles away from Long Island. Since Third Eye Books & Things will be a booth that mimics the same model of the street vendor market, Long Island customers will be familiar with the setup, and be able to purchase book titles at discount off-retail prices much closer to home.

1.2   Goals

- Make Third Eye Books & Things the premier location for Long Island residents to purchase African American books and natural healthcare products.
- Achieve a profitable return on investment within two years.
- Increase sales for Third Eye Publishing titles outside of the mainstream bookstores and street vendor market.

- Use the profits from Third Eye Books &Things to invest in printing machinery to create a Third Eye Publishing printing division so titles can be produced on demand.
- Within two years create a replica satellite Third Eye Books & Things at another flea market/mall location.

2.0   Company Summary

Third Eye Books & Things will be a Long Island retailer and distributor of Third Eye Publishing books, other African American titles, financial literacy material, and natural healthcare products and paraphernalia. The company will be formed as a division of Third Eye Publishing, Inc.

2.1   Company Ownership

Third Eye Publishing, Inc. has one principle owner—Therone Shellman. Third Eye Books & Things will have the same principle owner.

2.2   Projected Start-up Financial Plan
Start-up Requirements:

Store furniture (bookshelves, product stands, tables, counter) $2,500

Wireless credit card machine
$1,000

Equipment-Computer, cash register, fax machine, copier-scanner-phone $2,000

Inventory: books and products
$6,000

Computer software-inventory
$600

Marketing (business cards, postcards, local newspaper ads, newsletter) $1,000

Rent (one month/plus one month security)
$2,000-$4,000

Total Start-up Expenses

$15,100-$17,100

Start-up Assets:
Start-up Inventory: Three Third Eye Publishing titles
$3,000
Total Start-up Assets

$3,000

Immediate Liabilities:
Not applicable. Kiosks within flea market locations are covered under the flea market's insurance.

Total Start-up Expenses (from above)
$15,100-$17,100
Total Assets (from above):
$3,000
Total Loan Amount Needed:
$12,100-$14,100

2.3   Company Location and Facilities
Third Eye Books & Things will be located within a busy mall in Suffolk County or Nassau County, Long Island (New York). The mall is open seven days a week. People from all over Long Island and the county of Queens come to shop at this location since it houses the most jewelry centers within Long Island, as well as affordable clothing. The booth/kiosk will be the only one in the mall that sells books and natural soaps, oils, and skin care products.

3.0   Market Analysis Summary
According to online reports of book sales African American books represent one of the largest segment of growth within the book market. According to publishing industry experts, the trend is expected to continue, and reach, if not surpass, the financial

success in the hip-hop industry, which is in the trillions of dollars. Health is always a main concern for people, which makes the healthcare product industry a profitable industry in which to get involved. By combining the two markets of books and healthcare products at an outlet where people can feed their minds and take care of their skin and hair, Third Eye Books & Things will cater to a broad customer base that will extend beyond the African American market.

3.1   Target Market Segment Strategy

The target market profile is Long Island residents who represent many class and educational tiers. Most of the customer base travel considerable distances to purchase books and natural skin and healthcare products. These customers tend to be loyal to merchants who service all their needs at one location. This information I acquired by asking customers who purchased my own personal book titles at book signings. I used my book signings as a platform to do the research for my business plan and a guideline to what I need to do to create businesses which would service customers in the best way as possible.

Selling in Bulk Volume:
Much of this business needs to be cultivated through opportunistic networking, and diligent follow-ups of in-store inquiries and leads.

Interstate-shipments:
Interstate shipments will be contingent on expansion following the successful implementation of this business plan in the first year or two of operations. This business would develop through direct-mail catalog marketing (newsletter), and an Internet sales operation.

15

3.2   Market Needs

Little attention is paid to the opportunities that exist in Long Island concerning African American literature and natural health, skin, and hair products. Brooklyn, New York is the only borough larger than Long Island, so there is a strong market for these products. I've lived in Long Island most of my life. Suffolk County to be exact and I have never seen a book store which carried a multitude of African American literature. Even as I did my research and visited beauty supply stores I rarely came across stores which carried a large selection of natural skincare products such as soaps, lotions, body butters, etc. Here you will find hair care products which are made for African Americans.

3.3   Competition and Buying Patterns

Competition in the book and healthcare products combination market is to a large degree non-existent. Third Eye Books & Things will carry Third Eye Publishing's titles as well as other publishers' titles, ranging from children's books to financial wealth and spiritual literature. Titles will mainly be by African American authors. The healthcare products that will be sold include:

The first two Third Eye Publishing, Inc. titles have sold about 3,500 copies within the Long Island market to date. President and author, Therone Shellman, is very well known by readers and book purchasers in the Long Island area, most of whom will become store customers of Third Eye Books & Things.

4.0   Strategy and Implementation

Location is critical to attract the traffic and cus-tomer profile required to generate planned sales volumes. The malls represent the best retail opportunities because of their high volume of customer traffic. Three target areas were identified throughout Long Island.

Therone Shellman, President of Third Eye Publishing, is a seasoned executive management professional, having previously worked as a production supervisor for Nature's Bounty, Inc. He also authored Third Eye Publishing, Inc.'s first two titles. The first title, *Love Don't Live Here*, released in August 2006, became a best selling title On Booking Matters Magazine which conducts sales of African American titles within a select number of African American stores. The second title, *No Love Lost*, was an award winner in the African American Fiction category at the Indie Excellence Book Awards in 2007. This title was also a finalist in the African American Fiction Category for USABookNews.com. Shellman is also the co-author of *Love.com*, which released on December 15, 2007. From his various business experiences and endeavors, Shellman is knowledgeable in general business, sales, and book buyer habits.

4.1 Revenue Potential

Regarding Third Eye Publishing's titles, Third Eye Books & Things is forecasting average sales of eight hundred to one thousand books (ten dollars per book) for each title during the first year, four thousand to six thousand book sales (eight to fifteen dollars per book) from other publishers during the first year, and urban magazine sales of three hundred to six hundred copies (prices vary). Natural products—soaps, lotions, Shea butter, Muslim oils, and incense—will make up the bulk of the stores sales.

Sales Forecast:
Sales

	FY2008	FY2009	FY2010
Third Eye Publishing titles	$20,000	$35,000	$45,000
Other companies' titles	$40,000	$50,000	$60,000
Soaps, lotions, Shea butter, oils	$45,000	$50,000	$65,000
Posters, buttons, etc	$8,000	$12,000	$15,000

4.2   Sales Program

Third Eye Publishing, Inc. has an established Web site (www.thirdeyepublishing.org) and myspace accounts:

www.myspace.com/theroneshellman
www.myspace.com/thirdeyepublishinginc

A proprietary Web site will be created for Third Eye Books & Things to enhance customer service, supplier commerce, and direct sales. Peripheral sales and marketing collaterals (such as pens, refrigerator magnets, and buttons) will be used to expand product lines and customer awareness of the store.

Therone Shellman is an author with three published titles who has done signings at many bookstores. He knows how to present his merchandise in a professional and eye-catching manner. The booth layout for Third Eye Books & Things will be personally overseen by Shellman.

4.3   Strategic Alliance/Concluding Statement

Therone Shellman belongs to many writer and publisher organizations. Third Eye Books & Things will seek out opportunities to establish viable strategic alliances with authors, publishing companies, and community organizations. Third Eye Books & Things will enable Third Eye Publishing, Inc. to expand as a recognizable brand. Third Eye Publishing will then enable Third Eye Books & Things to flourish since the Third Eye Publishing's titles will provide a ready-made customer base for Third Eye Books & Things.

Part 3: Finding Capital for Your Business

There are many options to consider when looking for start-up capital for your business. It's a good idea to think things through and evaluate all your options before making any decisions.

A. Personal Savings
Most new businesses are financed primarily by the business owner's personal savings. Most owners will use their personal credit cards. Although your personal savings may be the easiest route to take, remember that most businesses fail because of a lack of resources. In most cases, a lack of knowledge and capital cause businesses to close within the first year.

B. Friends and Relatives
Your friends and relatives may lend you start-up money, and do so interest free or at a low interest rate, which can be a bonus. Every dollar saved when getting started is a big plus.

C. Banks and Credit Unions
If your business proposal is solid and thorough, then there is a very good chance for you to obtain a business loan. I will talk more about the different types of business loans below.

D. Venture Capital Firms
These firms do provide funding to some start-ups, but in most cases they help expanding companies grow in exchange for interest on the loan or partial ownership of the company.

Business Loans

Most people assume that it is very difficult to obtain a small business loan, but this is not always the case. If you have a felony on your record, then you may have some difficulty obtaining a loan. In that case, you may want to search for SBA programs where the qualifications are less strict. But other than that issue, a sound business loan proposal along with a good credit rating should get you in the door.

Requesting a loan when you do not have everything together is one of the main reasons why loan proposals are turned down. It means you're not prepared, and if you're not prepared, you're not going to be successful in business. Banks lend money to make money, not lose it. The better prepared and organized you are, the more successful you will be in obtaining a loan. You must know exactly how much capital you will request, how it will be used, and how it will be paid back.

Types of Business Loans

There are two basic types of loans: short-term and long-term. In most cases, a short-term loan has a life of up to twelve months. These loans are usually working capital loans, accounts-receivable loans, and lines of credit.

Long-term loans generally have a life span greater than one year and up to seven. Equipment and real estate loans have a life span of up to twenty-five years. Long-term loans are acquired for major business expenses such as purchasing facilities, furniture, and vehicles.

How Your Loan Proposal Will Be Analyzed

The first question a bank considers when a loan request is reviewed is how the borrower intends to pay back the loan. Lenders also want to know whether you are intending to invest some of your own capital to fund the business. In most cases lenders will not finance 100 percent of the business. Lenders also analyze your credit report, work history, and letters of recommendation to determine whether you are a sound candidate to pay back the loan. Some other questions lenders consider are the following:

- Do you have enough work experience and knowledge to run a business successfully?
- Does your loan proposal and business plan demonstrate your understanding of the business?
- Can the business make monthly payments based upon its cash flow demonstrated within the business plan?

Make sure you also consider each of these questions before approaching your lender for a loan. If you have positive answers to these questions, then you are more likely to get approved for your loan.

Small Business Association Financial Assistance Programs

The largest source of business financing in the U.S. is the Small Business Administration (SBA). The best way to determine if you qualify for one of the SBA's programs is to contact your local bank. The bank must be a qualified SBA lender. Or you can contact the SBA directly and speak to a loan officer. He or she can direct you to a lending institution which can assist you according to your business loan needs. If you have the time stop by your bank and ask to speak to their loan officer. You may need to set up an appointment because most banks have a loan officer which may handle either a few or several branches.

Once you get a chance to speak to them find out what SBA loans they participate in and what are the criteria of each. From there you're on your way.

Below are various loan programs offered by the SBA.

7(a) Loan Guaranty Program

The 7(a) Loan Guaranty Program is the SBA's primary loan program. Under this program the SBA reduces risk to lenders by guaranteeing a major portion of loans made to small businesses. This helps lenders provide loans to small businesses when funding in other cases is unavailable. This loan program should be a last resort option for owners trying to obtain funds. The eligibility requirements and credit criteria for the program are very broad, so they allow for many considerations in small business financing needs.

To qualify for an SBA 7(a) loan, a small business must meet the 7(a) criteria, and the lender must assert that it cannot provide the financing on reasonable terms except with assistance from the SBA. In most cases the maximum guarantee is seven hundred fifty thousand dollars. The SBA can guarantee as much as 80 percent on loans of up to one hundred thousand dollars, and 75 percent on loans of more than one hundred thousand dollars. There are other loan programs where the SBA guarantees more. Some of these programs are DELTA, 504 loan programs, and the International Trade program.

How It Happens

A small business applies to a lending institution for a loan; the lender reviews the application and decides if the business has all the necessary requirements to obtain financing on its own, or if it requires additional support in the form of an SBA guarantee. The lender then requires that the SBA back the loan. Under this program, the SBA guarantees the lender that in the event the borrower does not pay back the loan, the government will.

If the lender approves the loan based on an SBA guaranty, a copy of the application and a credit analysis are forwarded by the lender to the nearest SBA office. After SBA approval, the lending institution closes the loan and disburses the funds. You then make monthly loan payments directly to the lender. Repayment plans may be specially tailored to each business. There are no balloon payments, prepayment penalties, or application fees.

Financing Uses

Permitted uses for a 7(a) loan are very broad and include expanding or renovating facilities, purchasing machinery, equipment, and fixtures, improving the leasehold, financing receivables, keeping on-hand working capital, and refinancing existing debt.

Interest Rates, Fees, and Terms

The repayment length of time depends on how the proceeds are intended to be used, and the ability of the business to repay. Payment terms in most cases are five to ten years for working capital, and up to twenty-five years for fixed assets such as major renovation of real estate, or the purchase thereof. The purchase of equipment can also fall under fixed assets.

Both fixed and variable interest rates are available. For loans under fifty thousand dollars, rates may be slightly higher than 2.75 percent. But for loans with maturities under seven years, rates are somewhere around 2.25 percent. The SBA charges the lending institution a fee to provide the guaranty, and in most cases the lender passes this charge on to the borrower.

Collateral

Personal guarantees are required from all the principal owners of the business. Liens on personal assets of the owners may be required. In most cases a loan will not be declined where sufficient collateral is the only criteria not met. This is so because the SBA depending on the loan amount can guarantee up to 80 percent of the loan.

Eligibility

To be eligible for a 7(a) loan, the business must be operated for profit and fall within the size standards set by the SBA. A business is deemed a small business based on the average number of employees during a twelve-month period, or on sales averaged over three years. A manufacturing business can have from 500-1,500 employees, and a wholesaling business can have 1-100 employees.

What You Need for The Lender's Review

Documentation requirements may vary, so contact your lender for the specific information you must supply. Below is a list of some of the documentation and information you must provide.

1. Purpose of loan.
2. History of the business.
3. Amount of investment in business by owners.
4. Signed personal financial statements.
5. Personal resumes.
6. Financial statements for three years (existing businesses)

There are a number of specialized programs under 7(a) that address specific needs of new and established businesses. These specialized programs are all usually governed by the same rules, so make sure you speak to your lender or an SBA loan officer about your available options.

Low Documentation Loan (LowDoc)

One of the SBA's most popular loan programs is the LowDoc program. If you meet the requirements of your lender, LowDoc only requires a simple one-page SBA application form. The LowDoc is a way to get rapid approval for loans up to one hundred thousand dollars. For loans over fifty thousand dollars, you must also provide a copy of U.S. Income Tax Schedule C, or the front page of the corporate or partnership returns for the past three years.

The SBA guarantees up to 80 percent of the loan amount. Applications are usually processed within two to three business days. The funds cannot be used to repay most existing debt.

Fastrak

This program allows lenders to provide capital to businesses seeking loans up to one hundred thousand dollars without SBA approval. Lenders use their existing documents and procedures to make and service loans. The SBA guarantees up to 50 percent of a Fastrak loan. Maturities are usually five to seven years. Be aware that not all lenders participate in the Fastrak program.

CAPLines

Under this program there are five short term loans and revolving lines of credit for the working capital needs of businesses. CAPLines may be used to finance direct costs for construction needs, service supply contracts, finance direct costs associated with commercial and residential construction, and finance working capital by obtaining advances against inventory and accounts receivables.

International Trade Loan

This program is designed for businesses engaged in international trade, or those preparing to engage in international trade. This loan is for short-term and long-term financing. The SBA can guarantee up to $1.25 million for a combination of fixed asset financing and permanent working capital.

The Export Working Capital Program (EWCP)

The EWCP uses a one-page application form, and turnaround time is usually within ten days. This program was designed specifically for exporters seeking short-term working capital. The SBA guarantees up to 90 percent of the principal, and interest up to seven hundred fifty thousand dollars. You can also apply for a letter of prequalification from the SBA. A EWCP loan can combine with an international trade loan as long as the SBA's exposure is not above $1.25 million.

504 Certified Development Companies

These non-profit organizations are sponsored by private interests or by state and local governments. The SBA can cover as much as 40 percent of a 504 project up to $1 million. Proceeds from 504 loans must be used for fixed-asset projects such as purchasing land, construction of new facilities, renovation of existing facilities, or purchasing machinery and equipment. The 504 program cannot be used for working capital or inventory, or for repaying debt.

The 7(m) Microloan Program

This program provides small loans up to twenty-five thousand dollars. The average loan is ten thousand dollars. This is a pilot program available at a limited number of lenders. With this loan the SBA makes funds available to intermediary non-profit organizations, and in turn these organizations make loans to small businesses.

The Small Business Investment Company (SBIC)

SBICs are privately owned and managed investment firms that make capital available to small businesses through investments or loans. SBICs are for-profit firms whose purpose is to share in the success of a small business. The SBIC program is regulated by the SBA, and is designed for new or established businesses.

Women's Pre-Qualification Loan Program

Selected non-profit intermediaries work with applicants to develop a viable business plan and loan application. A loan request is then presented to the SBA, and in most cases a decision is made within three business days. Upon approval, the SBA provides a letter of prequalification. The applicant can then take this letter to a lending institution and apply for an SBA guaranteed loan of up to two hundred fifty thousand dollars. Contact your local SBA office to check for other requirements regarding approval.

The Minority Pre-Qualification Pilot Loan Program

This program utilizes local, private sector organizations as intermediaries to assist in the loan process. A prospective borrower works with the intermediary to develop a solid loan application. The application is then sent immediately to the SBA for consideration of a loan pre-qualification. Generally the loan application is for loans of two hundred fifty thousand dollars or less. Businesses that are 51% owned and managed by a racial or ethnic minority person(s), or not engaged in rental real estate are eligible.

Before you go into business, do your research. Contact your local branch of the Service Core of Retired Executives (SCORE). SCORE provides counseling and assistance on how to put together a business plan, and it will link you with someone who has previous work experience, or ownership of the type of business you would like to open. You may also contact the SBA for information on counseling and lending programs.

Part 4: Taxes

A. Employment Tax:

Every business except sole proprietorships is required to have an Employer Identification Number (EIN). Sole proprietorships are only required to have EINs if the sole proprietorship has employees. Also, in some cases, if the owners of sole proprietorships want to obtain a retirement plan, then they must also obtain an EIN.

Contact the Internal Revenue Service at 800-829-1040 to obtain information about getting an EIN. Or you can visit your local IRS office and request an SS-4 application form.

B. Sales Taxes

If you intend to sell products or services, you must register as a vendor. You're required to charge your customers sales tax, which you must remit to the state where you do business. In order to charge sales tax, you must be issued a Sales Tax Certificate of Authority. Through the certificate you are also allowed to issue resale certificates to purchase your goods for resale without paying back the sales tax.

Each state has its own information regarding businesses charging sales tax. You should research online at your state's Web site about how to obtain this information. For example for New York information, you can call the New York State Department of Taxation at 800-225-5829. To complete a form, ask for Form DTF-17. The New York State Department of Taxation's Publication 750 contains the application for registration as sales tax vendor. Each state has its own 1-800 number to obtain sales tax certificate information. Call your states department of taxation to find out what forms you need to fill out.

C. Federal Self-Employment Tax

If you are self-employed, your Social Security and Medicare contributions are made through the self-employment tax. Visit your local IRS office to receive publications and tax workshops, and to speak to a counselor. You can also contact the Internal Revenue Service at 800-829-1040.

D. Employee Taxes

All businesses with employees are required to pay various taxes and insurance. Some of these are:

(a) Social Security tax
(b) Medicare tax
(c) Federal Unemployment Tax (FUTA)
(d) NY State Unemployment Insurance Tax (or other state insurance, depending on where your business is located)
(e) Disability Insurance
(f) Workmen's Compensation Insurance

Other Rules and Regulations to Consider

Every business with employees is subject to comply with federal and state laws regarding the protection of employees. For example, NYSDOL **New York State Department of Labor** provides a free, on-site consultation program to advise business owners whether their facility and operations conform to Occupational and Safety Hazards Authority (OSHA) standards. The results of the consultation are not reported to OSHA, but serve to help owners conform to OSHA standards prior to an OSHA review. Each state has a department of labor. Contact your state department of labor, division of safety and health for more information regarding your state's programs. Each program may differ according to what state you reside in, but nevertheless all of them can provide you with up to date information on OSHA.

In addition, be aware of the Immigration and Naturalization Service's (INS) requirements. All employers are required to verify the employment eligibility of their employees. This regulation is governed under the Federal Immigration Reform and Control Act of 1986. All employers are required to process Employment Eligibility Verification Form I-9. Forms and an Employer Handbook are available from your local INS office.

Be sure to learn what government rules and regulations you are subject to before you open your business. Even though you may own your own business, and it may be small, most likely you will be subjected to some government rules and regulations.

Part 5: Marketing Your Business

There are two types of marketing. One is inbound and the other is outbound.

Inbound marketing is about knowing your product and potential customers, and how your product meets their needs. Pricing and packaging are key, as well as knowing your competitors. Branding is also important so that your product or service has a personality that is different than your competitors' products and services. Branding is when you create an image for yourself, organization or product which has an identity which is totally different than what other individuals, organizations or products represent.

Outbound marketing involves advertising, marketing, sales, and publicity focused on your organization. Customer service is key. Most of the time writers/publishers focus solely on outbound marketing. As a result, they strive to push their books onto people and organizations that really aren't interested in the product. Effective inbound marketing often produces more effective outbound marketing and sales.

A good example of enabling inbound marketing and outbound marketing to work together cohesively would be as with myself. As an author I utilize my books basically as a vehicle to market myself. In essence I'm the product, because I realize that all people have beliefs and views and are moved by them and the views, personality and beliefs of others which are similar to their own. All of my writing either revolves around social issues or are teaching others pertinent skills which they need to do their daily labor. This in itself is branding because most authors cling to the idea that they write books. This in itself is not unique at all because there are so many other individuals who write books. I on the other hand use my work as a tool to reach people who think like myself. I've created social network pages so we can stay connected. I also have an online radio show as well. All of my book covers have my personal myspace address on them. There are so many other marketing and advertising tools I utilize to bring attention to myself, my views and work.

Below are some of the tools and venues that can be used to market a product.

Targeted Mailing Lists

It's always good to utilize your local newspaper, or town or county papers to get the word out about your business. Most papers have advertising rates for flyers, postcards, and other mailings that can be placed inside the newspaper.

There are also companies that sell mailing lists, which can be tailored toward your customer demographics. For instance, if you are looking for women between the ages of twenty-forty-years-old who buy skincare products, then your mailing list can be tailored to reach these specific women. Some companies that sell skincare products collect demographic data on their customers, and then sell these mailing lists. Once you have the mailing list, you can now mail out your flyers and advertising material. This is a sure way to reach new customers who fall into your targeted demographic.

Business Cards

Many businesses such as Laundromats, delis, and local stores have community bulletin boards where you can place your business card for free. When starting a new business, you should take advantage of any free advertising opportunities.

Your business card should contain a company logo, a motto that reflects your company's purpose and vision if there is room to fit it on the card (our card doesn't have a motto), a Web site address or physical location (if you have both, use both), a phone number, and a fax number, if available. If you still have space on your card, a brief list of products or services you provide can also be included. Below is Third Eye Publishing, Inc.'s business card.

If you do not have a company logo there are plenty of companies which provide this service. Some of the ones I found on the internet are: At vistaprint.com you can create your own log for free. At getyourlogos.com you can view reviews of some companies which provide logo graphic services. I personally had the vision for the Third Eye Publishing logo because, I have the Eye of Osiris tattooed on the right side of my neck. One of my friends does graphics work so we searched the internet for Egyptian hieroglyphics and found the back ground we're using now. He touched it up a bit and this how we came up with the logo. So if you're a creative person you can think up a logo, draw it up, bring it to a graphic designer and let them finish it up. The Third Eye Publishing logo is below.

Coming up with a company motto may not be easy. But it should reflect the feeling you're trying to convey to people about your company. The Third Eye Publishing motto is "The Publishing House Where Knowledge Reigns Supreme". This statement sums up the message I'm seeking to convey about my writing and the works the company publishes. Yes, we want to entertain you. But most of all we want to enlighten you.

Cross Marketing

Cross marketing is important because you can utilize your products to market each other. For example, along with publishing my own book titles, I also sell natural skincare products of companies with whom I've developed distribution networks. Now whenever I attend book-signing events, I also bring along the skincare items. This product combination has worked out well, since selling the skincare products to my book-buying customers has been a success. This mainly because I sell more books to women then men.

Internet Marketing

The look and feel of your company's Web site will do a lot to help or hurt your business. If the home page is not visually appealing, then in most cases potential customers will not venture through the other pages on your Web site. The Web site should be easy to navigate and understand. Your ideas and product should stand out and convey a clear message. If you have a physical store location, then this information should be provided within one of the Web site's pages with store hours, a contact number, and maybe even information regarding a landmark if the business is located near a highway or within a shopping center. The easier you make it for people to contact you, the more likely they will. Convenience is always king in any business.

There are so many website designers that all you

have to do is do an internet search engine search and several pages will come up. I personally used HIT web solutions to design the Third Eye Publishing website. I like their page layouts because there is an administration section where you can go in and change wording, do updates to items and make so many more changes as needed. On the other hand if you're computer literate you can utilize yahoo site builder and build your own website. In fact the first site the company had was through yahoo site builder. I worked along with a friend and we built the site, page by page in two days. At the time I also utilized yahoo as the host. Currently we utilize HIT for hosting, so we make payments to the same source for the website domain name and hosting.

Before getting a website built ask around. Better yet visit websites and see if you like their look and feel. A lot of times at the bottom of the homepage is the name of the company who designed the website. You might want to shoot an email to someone at the company whose site you're visiting to see if they are satisfied with the website. I myself have gotten ripped off twice by website designers by looking up their names on the net, looking at their site, seeing how nice their site was then I hired them without finding out if they were credible. One designer told me at first it would only take her about two weeks to start and finish a site. After she received the money and the two weeks came, she then told me it would take a month more. The second graphics designer just bounced with the down payment altogether and he would not return my emails.

Choosing a look and feel for your website as well as the website designer shouldn't be a decision you make hurriedly. Take your time and do your research before hiring anyone.

Branding

It's not enough to manufacture a product and then think it will carry your company or brand. You must first consider what makes your product unique. Then the next thing to decide is how your product differs from other similar products on the market. How will it make customers eager to talk about it? When starting a new company, your advertising budget will be small, so you will depend on word of mouth advertising. You need to convey to customers the vision you have in regards to your product(s) and company. In other words what separates you and your product from others who may have similar products.

Social Networking Web sites

Social networking sites are a very good medium to access the public and speak to them about you and your company for free. I and Third Eye Publishing have about ten profiles on social networking sites, and within the pages of my profiles I link each site to the next so people have many ways to reach me. With the release of my first title "Love Don't Live Here" myspace.com was instrumental tremendously in helping me find and develop a following. I would post my book signing dates and locations as well as pertinent info about my myself, writings, and company. Social network sites are very effective because they allow you to reach out and be personal with people who may next door to you or thousands of miles away. I have a personal myspace page, an author page and a company page. I also have a facebook author page, blackplanet author page, tagged page, linkedin page, shelfari page, authorsnetwork page on ninn, Sister2Sister page, and about four other pages. I personally recommend social networking as a viable marketing tool. The downside to social networking is that you're up close and personal with people, so there is some hassles that come with this. I have stalkers, fans of other authors and authors themselves who have nothing better to do then seek to create some type of drama.

It also takes a lot of time to manage each site, so I do not answer every email I receive, nor do I participate in the games or add-ons that some of the sites have. So when a user sends me one of them requests I ignore it. I use the sites for business and network purposes and allocate maybe an hour every other day to them. They can become your life if you let them. It's not necessary to have as many social network sites as I do for myself and Third Eye Publishing. A few will do fine. The science behind what I do is that I'm not just branding the Third Eye Publishing name, I'm also branding my name as well.

Customer Service

Customer service is the most important aspect to a successful business when it comes to marketing, and it's also the most often poorly executed aspect of marketing.

For example when I receive an order for an item I ship it as soon as possible, in most cases the next business day. If I do not have a product which has been order I send the customer an email right away explaining I do not have the product and if they would like something else. There was one time where this happened and I sent the customer an email. They didn't respond back to me by the next day. So I immediately went online and sent their funds transfer back to them apologizing for not having the product. I'm almost certain that this was a company who provides ratings on companies customer service because they didn't respond. But nevertheless this is not the point. The point is that I did what I would like a company to do for me had I been in the same situation.

I have done a lot of book signings, and at one point I even had a location where I sold my company titles along with natural skincare items. Since I was always courteous and willing to explain at anytime details about an item I developed a strong customer base. Right now many of them are friends on my social network pages.

Part 6: Publicity

A. Radio and Television

The potential to attract customers via the radio and television is endless. Commercials are always a good medium in which to convey your product and message. But if you have a special product within a niche market, and you can find a radio or television outlet that caters specifically to your customer base, getting interviewed on air about the product or products you offer is great publicity.

The news, whether it's local or national, is always a great medium for exposure. In order to attract reporters' attention and make them want to interview you about your business, you have to tie the business happenings into an event that is newsworthy. For example, if you own a florist and decide that you will give away a free box of chocolate to the first one hundred customers who purchase a dozen red roses the day before Mother's Day, this event can be newsworthy. People are always interested in something free, and chocolates and flowers are always popular gifts for Mother's Day. So for any florist, Mother's Day is the perfect day around which to create an event and get local news attention.

B. Magazine and Newspaper Articles

Publicity is about utilizing mediums to reach large audiences. There is a magazine which caters to every product you can think of. This is a perfect medium to place an add about your product and reach a large audience. Not only this but people tend to read magazines more than once, and in many cases the magazine gets passed on and more than one person reads it. Newspaper articles are a very good way to reach thousands of people very quickly. If you can manage to get a write up in a big newspaper it has the potential to bring about a surplus of sales for your product(s) immediately. In some cases getting an article write up in the right newspaper has the same effect as being on radio or TV.

C. Speak Wherever You Go
Toot your own horn. Wherever you go talk about your vision and business. There is no one who can better convey what it is you offer, than you can.

D. National Exposure
The above information on publicity is for when your business is in its beginning stages. The next step is to get national exposure for your company Web site and company brand. Hire a publicist or publicity firm to help you with this.

E. Hiring a PR Person or Publicity Firm
Before hiring a publicity representative it's imperative that you understand the difference between someone who is a marketer and someone who is a PR person. If an individual or company cannot get you national exposure where you or your product has the opportunity to be viewed by several thousand or millions of people than this person or company is just a marketer. It's this simple.

When you're seeking a PR person or publicity firm check their track record and see who they've represented. A person or company can always be judged by the work they do. Most PR firms have a listing of the people and companies they've represented. Take the time to contact a few of the leads to see what they have to say.

Once you've found a rep or company your interested in having represent you ask to come in and have a sit down meeting. Have a notebook with questions. Below I have jotted down a few questions you should ask:

1. What areas of publicity are you experienced in?
2. What is the price range of a campaign? And do you work on a monthly retainer? Or do you charge by the services you provide?
3. In your honest opinion what areas of publicity do you think will suite me best?
4. How many individuals usually work on a campaign? (You ask this question because if more than one person is going to work on your campaign you want to make sure they are working in unison together so you get the most out of their efforts).

You may want to take the time to interview two-three PR reps and firms before making a decision on who to go with. This will be one of the most important decisions you will make so pay attention to the words which come out their mouth and the work they've done, as well as their experience and the knowledge they possess about how publicity works.

Part 7: Helpful Organizations and Associations

Therone Shellman Book Consulting
www.theroneshellman.com

Therone Shellman Book Consulting, is my business. Ever since I was thirteen-years-old, I had the entrepreneurial spirit within me. I want to dedicate part of my life to accumulating mental and physical wealth, as well as teaching others how to do the same. The company Web site will showcase my business material for you to purchase.

Keeping It Real
www.blogtalkradio.com/keepingitreal

Keeping It Real is an online radio show. I created this show to provide information on the self-publishing world, entrepreneurship, and community activism.

SCORE
www.score.org

SCORE is an organization composed of retired executives and business owners who are now volunteer business management counselors. The organization makes every effort to match a client's needs with a counselor who is experienced in the same type of business the client is seeking to open or currently owns. SCORE counselors meet with clients at a SCORE chapter office, an SBA office, or even at times at the client's place of business.

Any small business owner or client seeking to open a business can obtain counseling from SCORE. An idea is all that is necessary. Counseling before a business start up is a critical part of SCORE's operation.

Small Business Development Centers (SBDC)

www.sba.gov/sbdc

These centers are found on college campuses, and they are utilized to counsel and train small businesses in resolving organizational, financial, marketing, technical, and other problems that they may encounter.

SBA E-Business Institute

www.sba.gov/training

This online classroom is designed to bring easy online business courses to you twenty-four hours a day. It provides easily accessible courses on topics important to small businesses such as accounting, marketing, publicity, branding and much more.

Women's Business Center Program

www.onlinewbc.gov

Since 1979, the Office of Women's Business Ownership has helped women overcome the barriers they face in starting and growing businesses. The WBCP provides long-term counseling and training to women business owners around the country.

Veterans Business Development

www.sba.gov/vets/

The SBA offers veterans many services to help them make the transition from soldier to small business owner. Each SBA office has a designated veteran's business development officer.

Veterans' Business Outreach Program

The Veterans' Business Outreach Program (VBOP) exists to provide financial and technical assistance to veteran-owned small businesses.

Community Express Pilot Loan Program

This program is designed for new market small

businesses. These are businesses owned by minorities, women, and veterans, all of whom are underrepresented in the population of business owners compared to their representation in the overall population. Approved lenders are allowed to use an expedited loan review to process SBA guaranteed loans up to two hundred fifty thousand dollars.

Disaster Assistance

www.sba.gov/disaster

This loan is for long-range recovery for private-sector, non-agricultural disaster victims. Assistance is available to businesses of all sizes and to individuals. The following business loans also fall under the SBA's Disaster Assistance Program: Physical Disaster Business Loan and Economic Injury Disaster Loan.

If you would like your company's profile and address added to this book for future printings, just e-mail the information to admin@thirdeyepublishing.org.

Part 8: The Author's Personal Thoughts, Reminders, and Bewares

1.   I established Third Eye Publishing, Inc. in April 2005 with about twenty-four thousand dollars. I didn't want to take any shortcuts while forming the company, so I immediately established the company as an S Corp, paid the fees, and hired an accountant. Luckily I could do all the networking and company paperwork right from my apartment. I was living in a spacious two bedroom, so I turned one bedroom into an office. This worked out perfectly because it saved me money on rent, electric bills, and having to pay other expenses associated with a dedicated office space in another building. I mention all this because most people start their business with only a few months' store or office rent saved. To be safe when forecasting your business start-up needs, you should include about eight to twelve months rent and utilities, and any other expenses associated with running the business. Remember, most businesses fail within the first twelve months of operation because of a lack of cash flow.

2.   Take out the time to purchase accounting software for bookkeeping. I remember going to the accountant with a black notebook and a manila envelope filled with receipts. It was a total mess, and confusing to say the least. If I had taken fifteen to twenty minutes each day to input my information into an accounting software program, life would have been a whole lot easier for me when it came time to do taxes. Take heed, and add accounting software into your business plan and start-up budget.

3.   Develop a budget for every part of your business. Advertising, marketing, publicity, utilities

and day-to-day expenses should all have their own budget. The more organized you are with where your money goes, the more successful you will be with your business. I say this from personal experience. I watched thousands of dollars disappear due to various daily expenses that I didn't keep track of on a daily basis with clear and precise records. So don't make the same mistake as me. Every dollar counts, so make sure you know where each of your dollars are spent.

4.   You should always be mindful of the type of people you deal with, and who you're dealing with. Never underestimate anyone. As an entrepreneur, you should always be in charge of whatever you're doing. Take the time to learn the ins and outs of whatever business you undertake. This way you can always find the best options and solutions to your needs. People will try to put the squeeze on you if you let them. I had a problem with distribution when the company that was distributing Third Eye Publishing's titles went out of business. Another company bought out their contracts, and when I sought to get out of the relationship a few weeks after the transition, I couldn't. As it turned out the only person I was in contact with was a representative of the publisher. In order to get out of the contract, the company wanted me to pay some outrageous fees. I refused and decided that I was going to fight. After weighing my options, I decided to continue doing what I was doing outside the store market until they came to some reasonable terms I could agree with. In the end I got out the contract, but not before extensive damage was done to my company. For about six months my titles were not distributed to the stores, and I had no control over the online accounts like amazon.com.

I learned a valuable lesson from this experience. For starters, the day my distributor told me they were going out of business, I should have told them to release my titles instead of waiting to see how this new company was going to be. So if a company you're in business with dissolves, I recommend that you do thorough research about the new company, or immediately seek to release your company from any obligation to this new company. Do not wait to see how the new company is going to operate.

5.   Regarding branding, protect your company and personal image at all costs. Just like there are culture bandits, there are also individuals and companies that would love to steal your image and pass it off as if they thought of it themselves. I came into the publishing industry with a different message and purpose than any other African American male author. My first story, *Love Don't Live Here*, is about two young African American women who become single mothers through different circumstances. Both of these women are striving to raise their sons to be productive young men. I received a lot of negative feedback from certain sectors of the African American book market because many people thought I was being too preachy. Now in 2009, after I have campaigned all over the East Coast, and even in California, I see some new authors trying to preach my message. Most of these individuals would not have had the courage to deliver this message if I had not built the foundation for this type of open dialogue to be acceptable.

6.   I'm very aware that there are people who would like to get me out of the picture so that they can steal my identity. With this in mind, I make sure I only support certain events and keep my circle of friends very close. There is only one me, and I will do all I can to see that no one rides on the back of my

coattails. When you create your image, company vision, and brand, make sure you do the same. Make sure you stand by yourself in every way possible so people recognize the difference between you and your competitors.

7.   Keep the end in mind. A critical part of accomplishing this is to constantly reevaluate where you are. The best way to do this is to constantly update your business plan. Your business plan serves as a yardstick by which to measure whether your business objectives are sound and can be achieved.

8.   In the ever pursuit to brand myself I made the decision to close Third Eye Publishing and establish a venture which would utilize my name. So early 2011 Therone Shellman Book Consulting was formed. December, 2010 Therone Shellman Skincare & Distribution was established.

Part 9: Every Business Needs an Office

A good way to save money is to start your business out of your home, if possible. This is always a good way to save some cash. But as your business grows and you gain clients and vendors, or need a better business image or more room for productivity, you will need an office or warehouse space.

There are many office space options. You can lease your own space, seek out shared office space, rent a fully equipped office, or utilize a virtual office provided by companies such as Regus or Davinci Virtual Office Solutions.

If you choose to rent an office space on your own, you have the freedom to do whatever you want. But the downside is that you will most likely be stuck in a yearly lease. If you only need office space in a specific area for six months, then you will be paying an extra six months rent for nothing. You may run a contracting business and are doing a job in another state so you may need to set up an office somewhere until the job is finished. The other downside to renting your own space is that you will be footing the bill for all utilities. Sharing an office space can help defray some of these costs, but renting a fully equipped or virtual office provides an even better solution.

The greatest benefit to renting a fully equipped or virtual office through an office service provider is convenience. In most cases fully equipped offices can be rented for as little as one day per month, depending on the company with which you are working.

Virtual offices can be rented on a day to day or monthly basis, and they provide a low cost alternative for maintaining a professional image without the hassle of a physical office location. Some of the perks of a virtual office are having a permanent business address, a receptionist handling your calls, mail handling, and the use of a physical office whenever needed. There are also often professional meeting rooms, business lounges, videoconferencing suites as well as a business support team always on hand to act as your team. One disadvantage with a virtual office is that it does not provide storage space to house your inventory. If your business receives large shipments on a regular basis, you will need to have another location that can receive these shipments.

To find out more about fully-equipped and virtual offices, you can contact Regus at www.regus.com, 1-800-offices, or Davinci Virtual Office Solutions at www.davincivirtual.com, 1-888-voffice.

If none of these office space options work within your budget, at the least I recommend obtaining a PO Box at your local post office. With a PO Box you can have a consistent business address, and have your packages and mail forwarded to you wherever you choose.

Part 10: The Future of Your Business

Life and business is about moving forward, so you may need to enhance your education and networks to ensure that you come out on top. I've learned that some of the main ingredients to becoming successful are communication, education, and networking. And in some cases money has the ability to close the gap in other areas where you lack.

I wasn't born into generational wealth or a family-owned business, so I've had to learn things through trial and error. As with all businesses, start-ups are not just mentally taxing, but they are also financially taxing because you have to recoup your start-up costs if you can, and from there try to make a profit and build the foundation for your business. Most businesses not built from generational wealth will be the victim of mistakes. I believe that the potential for mistakes is what prevents many people with good business ideas from taking the chance of starting their own business.

Over 50 percent of new businesses fail during the first year. This scares people, and this fear is very understandable. But if you're like me and you realize that you were born to take chances, then starting your own business isn't so scary. Sometimes you will encounter failure, but there will always be success. And success comes from knowing what you're dealing with, and having the will to do what it takes to become successful. This starts with letting go of the fear of not being successful.

I grew up rough, without a mother or father. My sister and I went from foster home to foster home until we landed in one home and they adopted us. By the age of thirteen I realized we had to fend for ourselves, so I started working. I worked at a beer distributor in the bottle room and on warehouse floor.

In the summer I worked about forty-eight to sixty hours per week. And during the school year I worked forty to forty-eight hours each week. Having a job taught me about responsibility and having your own so I wouldn't have to depend on anyone else.

I don't know how much minimum wage was back then, but I was making a whole lot of money for someone my age. Unfortunately, no one ever taught me about financial literacy and how money accumulates. There is a science and formula to making money, and every successful entrepreneur has come to know the formula. The first step is to obtain as much knowledge as you can about being an entrepreneur. Knowledge is always the key to doing anything. The second step is to know the product or service you provide inside and out. Meaning its pros and cons. The third step is to know the demographics. Meaning the people who are in need of the product or services. The fourth step is to develop a marketing strategy to reach your potential clientele. The fifth step is to be able to provide and handle the need of the customers once the demand takes place. The sixth but one of the important steps is money management, managing the wealth you accumulate to grow your business to the point where you can get the ball rolling before bringing on investors. The seventh step is to bring in investors so you can utilize others peoples wealth to further your business goals. Think about it, huge corporations are the size they are because of investors and shareholders. Most very successful entrepreneurs are so successful because they utilize other peoples money to make more money, from there they share the profits. So for them it turns out to be all profit because they didn't invest any money.

In the streets I took notice that most of the big time hustlers had people fronting them material (drugs) on consignment, or they had investors who would invest their money along with theirs and in return they would obtain a percentage of the profits. But nevertheless the bottom line is that utilizing other peoples wealth will help you meet your goals a whole lot quicker than utilizing your own cash.

It wasn't until over a decade later when I became a hustler on the other side of the law that I learned this formula. But with this lifestyle, success came and went just like the seasons, because as long I couldn't integrate illegally earned money into the legal system, I couldn't build credit from my money, and I couldn't put large sums of my money into bank accounts to earn interest. Through my experiences as an entrepreneur on the wrong side of the law, I can assure you that entrepreneurship through legal means is the only way to get rich and stay rich.

Education

I'm always looking for opportunities to enhance what I do now and in the future. Since publishing my first book, I've done many speaking engagements at libraries and educational institutions. At these events I've been offered jobs by the administrators of the venues, but the first thing each one of these administrators ask me is if I have an undergraduate degree. When I tell them no, they look surprised because they realize that what I do is very technical. Not just anyone is able to self publish successfully or speak about many subjects with ease. Due to my lack of formal, advanced education, over the years I've missed out on the opportunity to be a history librarian and an administrator at a college, among other positions. So I do realize that with all the knowledge I possess, a simple piece of paper would validate my portfolio. After all, I am an entrepreneur, and it's always about exploiting every opportunity to make more money.

A friend told me one day, "You can have your company and continue to do what you do, plus you can have a job making close to six figures, not have to touch your company money, and be able to dump money into your company and other projects from your paycheck. Plus, when you get older, you can teach at a university as well as do lectures and get paid a lot of money. A degree will just add to all you bring to the table right now."

If you are an entrepreneur like me, the more education you get, the better off you will be, because you can always teach your knowledge to others and make a substantial income from teaching alone.

Real life experience, education, networking, and finances are all important aspects to becoming a successful entrepreneur.

At the time this work was coming to a close I had just finished reading "The Laws of Success" by Napoleon Hill. This book put all the missing pieces together for me. I now realized more than ever that I possessed all the knowledge I needed to pursue my definite aim. I may of not possessed a college degree, but neither did Henry Ford, and some of the other most powerful men and minds the world has ever witnessed. So for now on there would be no more looking back toward the past, because the past will never come back, today and the future is now and ahead of me. With this thinking I made the decision to move forward with branding my name and message. Therone Shellman Book Consulting, was formed to replace Third Eye Publishing with the publishing of my work. And in this regard the website address is none other than my complete name www.theroneshellman.com

Part 11: Conclusion

All The Information You Need To Know To Become An Entrepreneur is designed to give new entrepreneurs insight into how to formulate a plan to set up a business, and then execute that plan. Owning a business is about a lot more than just having a product or making money. There is a formula to success, and it all revolves around bettering the quality of people's lives. I don't care what type of product you sell, people should come first. Even if you sell dog leashes, it is people who decide that they actually want or need dog leashes to put on their dogs.

Entrepreneurship is also about a lot more than human greed. Spiritual wealth also comes into the equation. I say this because God wants us all to be prosperous. It is the reason why he gave us control over our lives, conditions, and circumstances. Otherwise he would have made us like puppets so he could pull our strings up and down to do whatever he wanted us to do.

As I wrote earlier, I was not born into generational wealth, nor did I grow up around anyone who could teach me the formula to success. I'm learning things as I go along, but I'm a quick learner, and I communicate very well, so I'm able to pass on what I've learned to you.

50 Cent has a movie titled *Get Rich or Die Tryin'*. I totally agree with this statement. If you're not spiritually rich, then you're not living to your full potential. If you're not physically wealthy, then you have not learned to manifest spiritual wealth into the physical world, and therefore you cannot truly inherit the wealth of this world.

I don't know about you, but the idea of being spiritually, mentally, and physically rich sounds very good to me. I will get there. Hopefully I will see you along my journey.

Glossary

Advantage: A condition, thing or event that can help or benefit.

Asset: A valuable quality or possession.

Disadvantage: A situation which is unfavorable.

Entrepreneur: A person who launches or manages a business venture.

Inbound Marketing: Inbound marketing is about knowing your product and potential customers, and how your product meets their needs. Pricing and packaging are key, as well as knowing your competitors. Branding is also important so that your product or service has a personality that is different than your competitors' products and services. Branding is when you create an image for yourself, organization or product which has an identity which is totally different than what other individuals, organizations or products represent.

Liability: The condition or state of being liable.

Marketing: Marketing is the ability to attract attention to oneself, organization or product(s). Business cards and fliers are considered aspects of marketing.

Outbound Marketing: Outbound marketing involves advertising, marketing, sales, and publicity focused on your organization. Customer service is key.

PR: Public Relations

Publicity: Publicity is the ability to utilize mediums to bring awareness to large audiences in regards to yourself, organizations or products(s). The TV, radio, newspaper and magazines as well as the internet can be at times mediums used to obtain publicity.

Revenue: Income returned by an investment.

SBA: Small Business Administration

About The Author

Therone Shellman was born in Brooklyn, New York, but was raised in Long Island, New York. He wrote his first novel *Love Don't Live Here* in 1990 while serving a four- to twelve-year prison sentence. In 2003 he self published the story, but realized he didn't possess all the necessary knowledge needed to become a successful author. After studying the industry for eighteen months he formed Third Eye Publishing, Inc and released the revised edition of *Love Don't Live Here*. The title to date has sold over sixteen thousand copies.

Therone Shellman is the author of Love Don't Live Here, No Love Lost, The Secrets of Self Publishing and the co-author of Love.com, and Survivor I Changed the Rules Part 1. www.theroneshellman.com

www.theroneshellmanskincare.com

Shea Butter* Mango Butter* Semi-Organic* Organic
PRODUCTS

Look For The **Therone Shellman Skincare & Distribution
Product Line**

www.theroneshellmanskincare.com